CRIME AND DETECTION

CYBER CRIME

Crime and Detection series

- Criminal Terminology
- Cyber Crime
- Daily Prison Life
- Death Row and Capital Punishment
- Domestic Crime
- Famous Prisons
- Famous Trials
- Forensic Science
- Government Intelligence Agencies
- Hate Crimes
- The History and Methods of Torture
- The History of Punishment
- International Terrorism
- Major Unsolved Crimes
- Organized Crime
- Protecting Yourself Against Criminals
- Race and Crime
- Serial Murders
- The United States Justice System
- The War Against Drugs

CRIME AND DETECTION

CYBER CRIME

ANDREW GRANT-ADAMSON

MASON CREST PUBLISHERS
www.masoncrest.com

Mason Crest Publishers Inc.
370 Reed Road
Broomall, PA 19008
(866) MCP-BOOK (toll free)
www.masoncrest.com

First printing

1 2 3 4 5 6 7 8 9 10

Library of Congress Cataloging-in-Publication Data on file at the Library of Congress

ISBN 1-59084-369-X

Editorial and design by
Amber Books Ltd.
Bradley's Close
74–77 White Lion Street
London N1 9PF
www.amberbooks.co.uk

Project Editor: Michael Spilling
Design: Floyd Sayers
Picture Research: Natasha Jones

Printed and bound in Malaysia

CONTENTS

Introduction 7

The Community Of Cyberspace 9

The Hackers 23

The Threat Inside 37

Business Under Attack 51

Virus Attack 65

Law Enforcement and Security 77

Glossary 90

Chronology 92

Further Information 94

Index 96

Introduction

From the moment in the Book of Genesis when Cain's envy of his brother Abel erupted into violence, crime has been an inescapable feature of human life. Every society ever known has had its own sense of how things ought to be, its deeply held views on how men and women should behave. Yet in every age there have been individuals ready to break these rules for their own advantage: they must be resisted if the community is to thrive.

This exciting and vividly illustrated new series sets out the history of crime and detection from the earliest times to the present day, from the empires of the ancient world to the towns and cities of the 21st century. From the commandments of the great religions to the theories of modern psychologists, it considers changing attitudes toward offenders and their actions. Contemporary crime is examined in its many different forms: everything from racial hatred to industrial espionage, from serial murder to drug trafficking, from international terrorism to domestic violence.

The series looks, too, at the work of those men and women entrusted with the task of overseeing and maintaining the law, from judges and court officials to police officers and other law enforcement agents. The tools and techniques at their disposal are described and vividly illustrated, and the ethical issues they face concisely and clearly explained.

All in all, the *Crime and Detection* series provides a comprehensive and accessible account of crime and detection, in theory and in practice, past and present.

CHARLIE FULLER

Executive Director, International Association of Undercover Officers

Left: In the movie *The Net* (1995), cyber crime is brought to the screen: Sandra Bullock (pictured) stars as a computer analyst who spends her days tracking down computer viruses until she is drawn into a web of deceit and murder by cyber criminals intent on stealing government secrets.

The Community of Cyberspace

Cyberspace is a new territory, a new dimension almost, in which we live and work. I have a question for a colleague who works in an office two doors down the hall. Once, I would have picked up the telephone, but now I use e-mail. The reply comes back minutes later. It turns out he is not in his office, but in Australia. I had not realized that, but it does not matter—we can do our business just as easily 12 yards or 12,000 miles apart. However, along with the benefits of new territory comes new crime.

OPENING UP NEW TERRITORIES

Not long after Christopher Columbus voyaged from Spain to the Americas, fortune hunters and pirates roamed the oceans to steal the gold that had been found there. Entrepreneurs persuaded the optimistic, or the gullible, to invest in new ventures that were doomed to fail. Investors in England poured money into a company that promised huge profits from trade with South America. The South Sea Bubble, the collapse of that business in the early 1700s, remains one of the most notorious corporate failures in history. In the new millennium, dot-com collapses echoed that disaster.

Opening up the West in the 19th century brought robbers, gambling, share swindles, and cattle rustling in its wake. Western movies celebrate the

Left: Never before has a new technology been taken up faster than the Internet. Driven by the World Wide Web, growth started to explode in the last decade of the 20th century, linking people in ways never contemplated (and never possible) before. The benefits are immense, but criminals have found opportunities, too.

Promises of riches beyond dream have always attracted investors. In London in the early 18th century, the South Sea Company collapsed, and the downfall of that business is remembered even today when we talk about the "bubble" bursting to describe dot-com failures.

Big sporting events, like the soccer World Cup, give a massive boost to betting organizations around the globe. Legal betting shops, like this one in Macao, face increasing competition from offshore Internet gambling, which can escape national laws and regulation, and is sometimes open to fraud and money laundering as funds move rapidly through cyberspace.

battles between good guys and bad guys. Without new technology, the West would not have been won so quickly: railroad and the telegraph made the rapid exploitation of a huge new territory possible. Nor would it have been won so quickly without the mavericks, those that rejected authority and cut corners. A fine line divides heroes and villains.

Cyberspace is also a new territory. As in the past, it is criminals who have been among the first to recognize the potential of a wide-open, sparsely populated, and poorly policed space. The crimes are similar, too. Theft, fraud, breaking and entering, vandalism, illegal betting, the sex trade, and investment scams are all a part of the Internet crime wave. Law enforcement agencies are fighting to keep up with an explosion of crimes that do not recognize international boundaries.

INTERNATIONAL COOPERATION

Police around the world have had to reinvent themselves as they battle against new kinds of criminals. They are up against something entirely new. The following is a true example. A Visa card was used by a man (myself) in an English village to buy software from a company in California. A **hacker** in an unknown location found the number of the credit card and sold it to another criminal in the U.S. It was then used to place bets totaling $6,000 with a betting Web site in Costa Rica. The Web site used a credit card merchant service in Montreal, Canada, to process its transactions. The Canadian business banked in Port of Spain, Trinidad. The Caribbean bank debited the card-issuing bank in Manchester, England. The computer at that bank was bright enough to recognize that I did not have a history of gambling and raised the alarm. Police in at least five countries could have an interest in the case, but how can they gather evidence? And where exactly was the crime committed?

Anyone given a blank piece of paper and asked to provide a solution to the policing of cyberspace would quickly come up with an answer: an international police force. However, such a force is not on the political agenda anywhere. The traditions of **jurisprudence** are too varied. Even countries that are apparently cooperating well and which have similar traditions experience difficulties.

For example, Europe does not have the same near-absolute attachment to freedom of speech as the U.S., where it is embodied in the Constitution through the Fourth Amendment. This became an issue when France wanted to ban access to Internet auctions of Nazi memorabilia. In Europe, there have been concerns about the possibility of providing evidence from computers that might help convict a terrorist in the United States, where he could face the death penalty. Most European countries will not assist in

THE RISE OF THE INTERNET COMMUNITY

Numbers online worldwide

Year	Number	% population
2002	544.2 m	8.96
2001	455.55 m	7.55
2000	280.86 m	4.63
1999	153.5 m	3.75
1998	119 m	2.91
1997	74 m	1.81
1996	55 m	1.31
1995	26 m	0.63

While the Internet has its roots in a network developed for the military and research institutions in the 1960s, it first became available to the public in the 1970s. But the breakthrough was the development of the World Wide Web by Tim Berners-Lee at Cern, the European particle physics lab, in 1989.

Internet traffic increased 25-fold between then and 1994. Then the most rapid rise in access to a new technology in world history started. While there is talk of near market saturation in North America, parts of Europe, and the Pacific Rim, much of the world still has few connections.

Source of figures: Nua Ltd., Dublin. (Figures from various survey companies vary considerably. Statistical methods used to compile the figures have also changed over the years.)

any trial that might end with capital punishment. Britain, for example, insists on a guarantee that the court will not impose a death sentence.

AN INTERNATIONAL SUCCESS STORY

Where there is agreement, law enforcement agencies are beginning to cooperate effectively. At the end of summer 2001, police in 12 countries carried out simultaneous raids to seize computers and arrest more than 200 people. Bob Packham, deputy director general of the British National Crime Squad, which coordinated the operation, said, "I am unaware of no other police operation that has pulled together so many law enforcement agencies worldwide to effect simultaneous raids and arrests."

Roy Penrose, Director General of the National Crime Squad for England and Wales, briefed the leaders of the world's richest nations at a G8 summit on the battle against cyber crime. His message was blunt: "Transnational organized crime is sophisticated and flexible. It abuses new computer technology."

The police claimed that they had broken the largest and most sophisticated pedophile group on the Internet. Indeed, more than a million images of children were found.

The story started five years earlier when a pornographic network in San Francisco revealed links to England. British police uncovered the Wonderland Club, whose members had to "pay" a joining fee of thousands of pictures. In the United States, 34 people were arrested in 31 cities.

Steven Ellis, from Norwich, England, was charged as a member of the Wonderland Club, but committed suicide before the trial. The sentences of between 12 and 30 months jail on seven other members of the "club" were criticized as "too lenient" by child welfare organizations.

Former FBI Director Louis J. Freeh (seen here in 1993 being sworn in) struggled to combat a massive increase in cyber crime following the development of the World Wide Web. He admitted the agency faced serious problems because of the rapid increase in computer crime.

U.S. Customs Commissioner Raymond Kelly said that anyone who thought they could hide behind a maze of **Internet Service Providers** (ISPs), servers, files, and screen names was wrong. "We will find them and bring them to justice," he said.

The 43 countries of the European Union, the U.S., Canada, and Japan have drawn up a Cybercrime Convention that seeks to bring the laws in these countries much more closely into line. It would also empower police to investigate on behalf of law enforcers in member countries. However, the Convention has its critics, particularly in the U.S., where there are strong concerns that it threatens freedom of speech.

CATEGORIZING CYBER CRIME

There is general agreement about the categories of **cyber crime**. Louis J. Freeh, former director of the FBI, outlined them at the Senate Committee on Appropriations at the start of the new millennium. He warned that the fight against cyber crime was an uphill battle. He gave figures on investigations into intrusions ("hacks" in everyday language) and said, "In short, even though we have markedly improved our capabilities to fight cyber-intrusions, the problem is growing even faster and thus, we are falling further behind. These figures do not even include other types of crimes committed by a computer [user], such as Internet fraud or child pornography online." He identified 10 main areas of cyber crime:

• Insider threat—The **disgruntled** insider is a principal source of computer crime. More than half the businesses and organizations responding to a survey reported malicious activity by employees or those who had been employees until shortly before the attack.

• Hackers—Sometimes, hackers crack networks simply for the thrill of the challenge and to brag about it. Recently, there has been a rise in cases of hacking for illicit financial gain or other malicious purposes.

• Hacktivism—Politically motivated attacks are placed on publicly accessible Web pages and e-mail servers to send a political message. An example was the "Electronic Disturbance Theater," which called for civil disobedience online to support the Zapista movement in Mexico. Supporters of hacker Kevin Mitnick hacked the Senate Web site and defaced it.

• Virus writers—Viruses pose an increasingly serious threat to networks and systems worldwide. A good example of the response to virus writers was the arrest within a few days of the writer of the Melissa virus that was said to have caused $80 million in damage in 1999 (see pages 67–73).

• Criminal groups—The FBI was seeing the increased use of cyber-intrusions by criminal groups who attack systems for monetary gain. In the Phonemasters case (see pages 51–53), new data-wiretapping technology was used for the first time to gather evidence against a gang that cost businesses $1.85 million.

• Distributed denial of service attacks (DDOS attacks)—These are attacks that flood Internet servers with information that requires a response, thus causing servers to crash or slow traffic to a crawl. Many leading Internet companies, including Yahoo!, have been subject to DDOS attacks.

• Terrorists—Terrorists are known to use information technology and the Internet to formulate plans, raise funds, spread propaganda, and communicate securely. An example was a successful denial of service attack on Sri Lankan government servers by the Internet Black Tigers. (Since the attacks of September 11, 2001, much attention has been given to the use of the Internet by terrorists.)

• Foreign intelligence services—In a case dating back 15 years, known as The Cuckoo's Egg, West German hackers were able to penetrate computers in the United States, Western Europe, and Japan, and then sell sensitive information to the Soviet Union. Freeh told the Senate Committee, "While I cannot go into specifics about the situation today in an open hearing, it is clear that foreign intelligence services increasingly view computer intrusions as a useful tool for acquiring sensitive U.S. government and private-sector information."

It was the Canadian Mounties who tracked Raphael Gray to his home in west Wales. He had hacked into Internet shopping sites around the world and stolen the credit card details of 23,000 people. The FBI said his activities could have cost $3 million. The judge who sentenced Gray to three years community rehabilitation with psychiatric care said he had shown a "sense of humor" by using a stolen credit card number to send Viagra tablets to Microsoft boss Bill Gates.

CYBERCRIME CONVENTION

In the fall of 2001, 31 nations signed the Cybercrime Convention, drawn up by the Council of Europe. Signatories outside Europe are the United States, Canada, Japan, and South Africa. The Convention covers three main topics: harmonization of national laws, prosecution procedures to cope with global networks, and rapid and effective international cooperation. There are four main categories of offenses:

1. Offenses against the confidentiality, integrity, and availability of computer data and systems.
2. Computer-related offenses, such as forgery and computer fraud.
3. Content-related offenses, such as the production, dissemination, and possession of child pornography; a section on the propagation of racist and xenophobic ideas was to be added.
4. Offenses related to infringement of copyright and related rights; the wide-scale distribution of pirated copies of protected works, and so on.

NEW PROCEDURES

The Convention embodies basic rules that will make it easier for the police to investigate computer crimes. To protect human rights, these rules are subject to conditions and safeguards in the laws of member states.

INTERNATIONAL COOPERATION

Police in one country will be able to collect computer-based evidence for police in another, although they will not be able to conduct investigations or searches across borders. Information obtained must be passed on rapidly.

• Sensitive intrusions—In recent years, there has been a series of intrusions into Department of Defense computer networks, as well as those of other federal agencies, universities, and private-sector entities. Senators heard that "enormous amounts of unclassified but sensitive information had been taken." The intrusions appeared to originate in Russia (see pages 54–58).

• Information warfare—Foreign militaries' use of computers to wage war was called "one of the greatest potential threats to national security." The hearing was told that several nations were developing information-warfare programs because they believed the United States' reliance on information technology was its weak spot.

The fight against cyber crime has moved to the heart of government. The National Security Council, whose White House situation room is pictured here, has taken a leading role in the battle, and one of its top officials, Richard Clarke, was chosen by President Bush as his special adviser on cyber security.

The Hackers

Early hackers were heroes. They were the men who made the computer revolution happen. They worked in places like the Massachusetts Institute of Technology Artificial Intelligence Lab. This was one of the places linked to the Arpanet, the forerunner of the Internet, shortly after its foundation in 1969. Xerox's famed Palo Alto research center was another lab where hackers worked. Palo Alto was a powerhouse of ideas that influenced the way computers were to be used. The mouse, icons, and windows—the graphic user interface (GUI)—all came from there.

HACKERS—REAL AND IMAGINARY

Seymour Cray, designer of the supercomputers that carried his name, was a hacker. His machines transformed weather forecasting and were widely used by governments for breaking codes and analysis.

Dennis Ritchie and Ken Thompson of the Bell Labs' computer science group, created Unix, the operating system for minicomputers. Unix servers continue to provide much of the backbone of the Web. Richard Stallman got a job at MIT's artificial intelligence lab while he was still an undergraduate at Harvard. He did not believe software should be private property and founded the Free Software Foundation. These men were typical of the early hackers. They could make computers do things that others could not imagine and were driving the revolution.

Then, in 1984, came the movie *War Games,* in which teenager David Lightman (played by Matthew Broderick) hacks into a computer and starts playing Global Thermonuclear War. To him, this is just a game, but the

Left: Ping...the complex route a message has taken from the other side of the world on the information superhighway flashes up on the screen. Most users just want their computer to work. But others want to know how it works; they are the hackers. Increasingly, they are also criminals.

In 1984, the film *War Games* brought into question the relationship between people, computers, and decisions about nuclear war. Here, the hero David Lightman, played by Matthew Broderick, works at the home computer he uses to hack the National Defense System.

computer, War Operational Research, is interested in more serious games. It is a part of the U.S. National Defense System, and David is actually playing with a simulation of nuclear war. He triggers a national emergency that raises questions about the relationship of humans and computers. The futuristic sets added to the glamor of what David found himself doing. *War Games* is credited with igniting the interest of teenage boys—and it is mostly boys—in hacking. They found breaking into computers a challenge, and some went beyond that, causing real damage.

SO WHAT IS HACKING?

Webster's Collegiate Dictionary gives two computer-related meanings to the word "hacker." The first is "an expert at programing and solving problems with a computer." The second is "a person who illegally gains access to and sometimes tampers with information in a computer system." The second meaning has come to dominate, although old-style hackers are resentful at the misuse of the word.

Hacking costs businesses, government agencies, and other organizations worldwide huge sums of money. How much is impossible to judge because many incidents go unreported. The 2002 computer crime and security survey for the Computer Security Institute (CSI) and the FBI showed that 4 out of 10 organizations surveyed had their systems penetrated from the outside in the previous year. Average losses, for those who were able to quantify them, were more than $226,000. The threat from hackers is

SECRETS OF THE LITTLE BLUE BOX

Thirty years ago, the world reveled in the story of John Draper, who chose the pseudonym "Cap'n Crunch" to hide his identity. He found a toy whistle in a packet of the breakfast cereal and realized it produced the 2600-hertz tone needed to access phone lines. He made a little blue box to generate the dialing tones to make free long-distance calls.

Esquire magazine brought him fame with an article entitled, "Secrets of the Little Blue Box." If it was not for that publicity, he might never have gone to jail. The article led to an international following, including college kids Steve Wozniak and Steve Jobs, who went on to found Apple Computers. Free calls lasted until phone companies updated their systems. *Newsweek* many years later put Cap'n Crunch in their top-20 list of hackers.

increasing according to the report and has been for the past five years.

The FBI sees hacking as an increasingly serious crime. As the Internet has expanded, so have the opportunities for hacking—more people with computers at home means more targets. Criminals who are out to steal money, secrets, and the identities of other people have overtaken teenagers as the main threat in the eyes of law enforcement agencies. Identity theft—pretending to be someone else by stealing their personal information, such as name, date of birth, social security number (SSN), and credit card details—has been called the crime of the new millennium. Identity thieves use old-fashioned methods like Dumpster-diving and street robbery, as well as hacking computer databases for information. In 1999, the Social Security Administration's fraud hotline received 62,000 complaints of SSN misuse, and the trend continues upward. The cost to banks and their customers runs into hundreds of millions (if not billions) of dollars a year. Organized crime syndicates are believed to be behind much of this crime wave, drug traffickers in particular.

THE FIRST FEDERAL COMPUTER CASE AGAINST A JUVENILE

Against this background, police around the world have lost patience with teenage hackers. At 9:00 A.M. on March 10, 1997, phones were cut off at Worcester Airport in Massachusetts. The control tower and the fire department were cut off. The main radio at the tower would not work. After six- and-a-half hours, the system started operating again. At almost the same time as airport communications were restored, the whole phone system in Rutland, Massachusetts, went down. U.S. Secret Service Acting Special Agent in Charge Michael T. Johnston said, "This case, with the associated national security ramifications, is one of the most significant computer-fraud investigations conducted by the U.S. Secret Service."

The attack showed the vulnerability of thousands of similar telephone-company computers across the country. These loop-carrier systems integrate voice and data coming down copper phone lines for transmission

over a sophisticated fiber-optic cable. "Just as disabling a circuit breaker box blacks out an entire house, so disabling a loop-carrier system cut off all communications with the telephone lines it services," explained U.S. Attorney Donald K. Stern.

The hacker was a teenage boy who, under federal law, cannot be named. It was the first computer crime case brought against a juvenile under

Right: One of thousands of computer hackers at the Beyond Hope (Hackers on Planet Earth) convention in New York. Many hackers see themselves as "white hats" that expose the failures of computer companies to make their products secure. "Black hats" are the criminal hackers, but the distinction is less and less recognized by the law.

federal law. Attorney Stern said: "Computer and telephone networks are at the heart of vital services provided by the government and private industry, and are critical infrastructure. They are not toys for the entertainment of teenagers. Hacking a computer or telephone network can create a tremendous risk to the public.... This case reflects our intention to prosecute in a federal court anyone, including a teenager, who commits a serious computer crime." The teenager was put on probation and banned from remotely accessing a computer for two years. He was also ordered to pay **restitution** to the phone company and complete 250 hours of community service. His computer was confiscated.

Here, a group of teenage would-be hackers compare notes at the H2K2 Conference in New York City, July 2002. The three-day conference attracted an estimated 2,000 security professionals and computer activists. Some of the world's best-known hackers unveiled a plan to offer free software to promote anonymous Web surfing in countries where the Internet is censored.

THE ARTICLE THAT CHANGED HISTORY

"A magazine article that got me interested in phone phreaking long ago…was labeled "Fiction" in *Esquire* magazine, but it turned out to be real," says Steve Wozniak—founder, along with Steve Jobs (pictured), of Apple Computers—on his Web site, www.woz.org. The article, about Cap'n Crunch, started:

"I am in the expensively furnished living room of Al Gilbertson (his real name has been changed), the creator of the 'blue box.' Gilbertson is holding one of his shiny black-and-silver 'blue boxes' comfortably in the palm of his hand, pointing out the 13 little red push buttons sticking up from the console. He is dancing his fingers over the buttons, tapping out discordant beeping electronic jingles. He is trying to explain to me how his little blue box does nothing less than place the entire telephone system of the world, satellites, cables, and all, at the service of the blue-box operator, free of charge…. You can call yourself from one pay phone all the way around the world to a pay phone next to you. And you get your dime back, too."

THE CUCKOO'S EGG CASE

A problem facing law enforcement agencies is finding out where an attack comes from. Is it a foreign intelligence agency, commercial espionage, criminals trying to steal money, or teenage hackers out for the buzz? The government is reluctant to talk about espionage, but there can be no doubt that it happens. In 1989, Clifford Stoll, a systems administrator at the University of California, Berkley, found a discrepancy of just 75 cents in an account. He set about finding the reason, and it led him to a West German gang of hackers. He tells the story in his best-selling book, *The Cuckoo's Egg.* It soon became clear that many military, science, and industry computers in the U.S., Western Europe, and Japan had been penetrated. The trail led to West Germany (before reunification) and a gang of hackers. They were stealing **passwords**, programs, and other information that they sold to the Soviet KGB. Three members of the gang were sentenced to time in prison.

A year after the Cuckoo's Egg case, intrusions into more than 500 military and civilian government computers and private systems were discovered. Operation Solar Sunrise was launched in response. At least 200 unclassified military systems were penetrated, including seven Air Force bases, four Navy installations, and the Department of Energy National Laboratories. A 24-hour guard was placed on all military computers to detect and stop intrusions.

The attacks were happening as the military buildup for the Gulf War was taking place. Links to some Gulf region Internet Service Providers heightened fears that Iraq was behind the attack. A huge interagency investigation was launched. For four days, the government did not know who was attacking key defense computers essential to deploying forces in the Gulf. The trail led to two high school students in Colverdale, California. They had learned their skills from 20-year-old Ehud Tenebaum, an Israeli hacker known as "The Analyzer," who was passing on his knowledge before retiring. He also had four Israeli pupils.

THE DATASTREAM COWBOY AND KUJI

In 1994, U.S. agents sat in a bunker and watched as a hacker signed on to a computer using the user name of a high-ranking Pentagon employee. As

The elusive Kuji: working with the Datastream Cowboy, he was seen as the number-one threat to U.S. security because he probed secret sites in both America and the Far East. But he was untraceable as he launched attacks from three continents. Two years later he was uncovered.

Hero or villain? Kevin Mitnick, America's most famous hacker, was once on the FBI's Most Wanted List. But some people think he fell victim to an overbearing state that got his activities over two decades out of proportion. He is pictured in 1995, the year he was jailed for 14 months.

the "Datastream Cowboy" went through battlefield simulation data, artificial intelligence files, and reports on Gulf War weapons, the agents' fingers flashed across their keyboards in an attempt to identify the hacker. However, they could not even establish in which country he (or she) was sitting.

When he left the Pentagon computer, the agents "followed" him and watched, horrified, as he tried to get access to a nuclear facility in Korea. They feared the attack would appear to be coming from a Pentagon computer and that Communist North Korea would see it as an American attack. However, the target was in South Korea. In a few weeks, the Datastream Cowboy had become the number-one threat to U.S. security. He was working with an even more accomplished hacker called Kuji. They were untraceable, going though computers in South Africa, Mexico, and Europe before launching their attacks. In less than four weeks, the Datastream Cowboy and Kuji entered the Rome Laboratory, at the Griffiss Air Base in New York State, 150 times.

THE HACKERS ARE FINALLY TRACED

Eventually, it was old-fashioned police work that identified the Cowboy. An informant who surfed the Net discovered that the Datastream Cowboy's cyberspace hangout was at an ISP in Seattle. The informant chatted with him and before long, found out he lived in England. The Cowboy even gave the informant his phone number.

Scotland Yard's computer crime unit then traced him to a house in a dreary north London suburb. Telephone traces revealed he was dialing Bogota, Colombia, and from there, using a free phone line to hack into the military sites. The Datastream Cowboy was not a dangerous spy, but a 16-year-old music student named Richard Pryce, who had barely scraped through his computer science exam at school.

It was two years before Kuji was discovered. He was Matthew Bevan, a 21-year-old computer worker in an insurance office in Cardiff, Wales, whose bedroom was covered with *X-Files* posters. Pryce later told *The Sunday Times* of London, "It was just fame, a challenge. I was amazed how good I got at it. It escalated very quickly from being able to hack a low-profile computer, like a university, to being able to hack a military system."

Pryce was fined £1,200 (about $2,000) after his lawyer insisted it was an exaggeration when the Senate Armed Services Committee was told that he had caused more damage than the KGB and was the "number one threat to U.S. security." A charge of conspiracy against Pryce and Bevan was dropped, and Bevan walked free.

AMERICA'S MOST FAMOUS HACKER

Most young hackers grow out of it, as Pryce has. But not Kevin Mitnick, America's most famous hacker and once on the FBI's Most Wanted List. He started out stealing computer manuals from Pacific Bell in Los Angeles and kept going. His grandmother said, "He's got a very curious mind. He's never destroyed anything. He loves technology; he wouldn't hurt it." And his attorney, Donald Randolph, said, "He's a recreational hacker. He didn't do it for economic gain or damage anything, and there's no allegation he attempted to damage anything."

That has not made Mitnick any more popular with the law enforcement agencies. He has been held in the Los Angeles Metropolitan Detention Center, where violent criminals are often held. The U.S. Supreme Court has turned down his appeals for bail twice. Mitnick has been charged and sentenced seven times.

He first gained national notoriety in 1982, when he hacked into the North American Defense Command (NORAD), an escapade said to have inspired the movie *War Games*. However, he was not charged with that. In his early days, he also gained control of telephone offices in New York and California, also without charges following. He first went to jail after hacking into Digital Equipment Corporation computers.

In 1992, subject to a federal arrest warrant, Mitnick became a fugitive.

He went on a hacking spree, but was traced by a computer expert who discovered that his home computer had been hacked.

Mitnick was held in custody for three years before a plea bargain in 1999 put him into prison for another year. His case generated enormous interest, with a Free Kevin Mitnick Web site and stickers. Steve Gold, news editor of *Secure Computing* said: "For all he's done, there are despots and murderers out there who have suffered less than Kevin."

Supporters of Mitnick hacked into the Senate Web page and defaced it. Such action is what is now being called hacktivism. And that is the problem for the authorities in handling hacking. Being on the receiving end of a hack, you do not know at first if it is coming from terrorists, spies, criminal gangs, or teenagers honing their computer skills.

KEVIN MITNICK'S RECORD

1981: Computer fraud; one year probation (California)

1987: Computer fraud; sentence unknown (California)

1989: Hacked into MCI and Digital Equipment computers; one year in low-security prison (partly at a halfway house for people with compulsive disorders) and three years supervised release (California)

1992: Hacked into Department of Motor Vehicles computers; charges still pending (California)

1995: Possession of unauthorized access devices; eight months in jail (North Carolina)

1995: Violation of supervised release; 14 months in jail (California)

1996: (came to trial 1999): Computer fraud, wire fraud, and possession of unauthorized access devices; held in custody from arrest to trial and sentenced to a further year in jail.

The Threat Inside

"Revenge is a kind of wild justice, which the more man's nature runs to, the more ought law to weed it out," the English essayist Francis Bacon wrote in the 17th century. To today's police, it is a thoroughly modern sentiment, as disgruntled employees increasingly use computers to take revenge. A few years ago, someone who felt he or she had been unfairly fired might drop an important file behind a cupboard. Now, he or she can set a computer time bomb if skilled enough, or send a damaging e-mail to customers if not.

BEWARE THE DISGRUNTLED EMPLOYEE

Insider computer crime includes both revenge and fraud. Many of these crimes go unreported because companies and government agencies are reluctant to admit that their systems are not as secure as they would like the world to believe. Disgruntled employees have been considered the biggest cyber crime threat, although there are signs that external attacks are overtaking them as access through the Internet increases.

High-tech businesses are the most vulnerable because many of their employees have the skills they need to hack the system. When the dot-com bubble burst at the start of the millennium and staff were laid off, federal investigators noticed a rise in revenge attacks.

"The whole nature of computer crimes has changed. The problem at big companies is [that] the network administrator is probably the last guy who finds out you got fired, and doesn't cut off your access. Or it's the network administrator who gets fired, and he has access," said Agent Greg Walton

Left: It could be anyone—the most unassuming man or woman in the workplace might be plotting to damage the company. It is often easy to obtain someone else's password and gain entry to an organization's most sensitive data.

People who work late and alone in an office are often among the first suspects when an insider crime is detected. Increasingly, security systems are used to record when employees are in sensitive areas of office and factory buildings.

of the FBI's San Francisco area computer intrusion squad.

Many employers have set up policies to prevent revenge attacks. When someone is fired, this person is immediately escorted from the building and his or her belongings are sent afterward. The system administrator is informed immediately, and the ex-worker's computer access is stopped. This works as long as the password system is secure, but frequently, people give their passwords to colleagues. It is often the easy and practical way to work. A document is urgently needed, but it is on the computer of someone who has the day off. Rather than come into the office, this person gives the password to a colleague. Or, some write their passwords on the bottom of their keyboards. There is a mismatch between the way people interact at work and the needs of computer security.

Sometimes, the damage is more embarrassing than anything else. One former contract employee at a technology company hacked the computer and sent e-mails, pretending that these were from management. They told workers the company was going out of business, and the messages also had a pornographic attachment.

EXPERT CYBER SABOTAGE

The expert can cause damage that may bring a business to its knees. This is the story of an attack so complex that it took investigators years to discover how it had been done.

Starting the computer server was the first job of the day for the first person to arrive at the manufacturing facility of Omega at Bridgeport, New Jersey. On July 31, 1996, a message stating that a section of the file server was being fixed appeared on the screen. Then the server crashed. The backup tape could not be found. Then it was discovered that the server had not just crashed—more than 1,000 programs needed to make 25,000 products had disappeared. Omega, with headquarters in Stamford, Connecticut, makes high-tech measurement equipment and instrumentation. Before the Omega case was solved, 80 people had lost their jobs, the company had lost $10 million, and growth plans for the company had been derailed.

Suspicion centered on Tim Lloyd, the 37-year-old who, in 11 years with the company, had risen from the machine room to become chief computer network program designer. Tim Lloyd had been fired three weeks before the crash. But if the crash was the result of a crime, how had it been carried out? The Secret Service was called in under a law that makes computer sabotage a federal offense if it causes more than $5,000 damage and affects a computer used in interstate commerce. Special Agent William D. Hoffman started an investigation that would last four years.

The job of finding clues on the hard disk was given to Greg Olson of Ontrack, a data recovery and computer forensics business. "I've never seen this massive a deletion in my 10 years of experience," he said. Eventually, he pieced together odd bits of code and found lines of commands timed to operate on July 31, 1996. Normal deletion code had been modified to replace the normal "deleting" screen message with "fixing." Then, Olson found the same code on one of Tim Lloyd's hard disks.

The jury found Lloyd, who continued to maintain his innocence, guilty of setting up one of the biggest computer "time bombs" ever. He was jailed for 41 months.

"BILLION-DOLLAR BUBBLE"

Large-scale employee fraud has always been a threat to business. Yet, how much of it should be classified as cyber crime? Today, virtually everything that happens in a business involves computers so, inevitably, an employee working a scam on the firm is aided by electronics. This next case dates from the early 1970s, long before the term "cyber crime" had been coined, but it could not have been on the same scale without a computer. That is what makes the "Billion-Dollar Bubble" significant in the history of cyber crime, as well as a spectacular event.

Executives at Equity Funding set up 64,000 fake insurance policies.

Monitoring of communications networks plays a crucial part in the investigation of computer crimes. If people and transfers of information can be associated, this will often provide the evidence that investigators need before questioning a suspect.

Computer forensics experts employed by the police can often find information that computer users thought they had completely erased when trying to cover their tracks. It is very difficult to conceal the use anyone has made of a computer system.

THE CYBER-EMBEZZLER

It was old-fashioned police work—putting two bits of information together and seeing a crime—that uncovered a cyber-embezzler. A police raid on a bookmaker revealed the unusual betting habits of one man. The man, Roswell Steffen, was a teller who trained new tellers at the Union Dime Savings Bank in New York. Steffen earned a moderate salary, yet placed bets of $30,000 a day. The bank found it difficult to believe, but when bank investigators went through the books, they found Steffan had embezzled $1.4 million. He had a computer terminal with supervisory access and two cash boxes, one containing $10,000 and the other $50,000. He had started by borrowing $5,000 from the cash fund with the intention of repaying from his winnings. When that was exhausted, he borrowed more and had no prospect of repaying it.

For three years, Steffan used a range of tricks to get money. These included reducing deposits made by customers and creating new accounts. Eventually, he was juggling 50 accounts. He made frequent mistakes, yet he was not caught because when auditors found discrepancies he would simply blame them on the inexperience of the tellers he was training and use his supervisory terminal to make corrections.

They then sold these policies to other insurance companies in re-insurance deals. That brought in cash in the first year, but premiums had to be paid to the re-insurance companies in the second year. So more fake policies were created and sold to pay for the premiums. And thus the cycle went on for more than 10 years until the fraud was uncovered in 1973.

By this time, the task of preparing bogus policies was so great that a computer program had been written to generate policies. By the time the whistle was finally blown by an employee who had been fired, 70 percent of Equity Funding's policies were bogus.

COMPLEX CRIMES

Accountants Geoffrey Osowski, aged 30, and Wilson Tang, aged 35, worked for Cisco Systems in California. The charges they faced are a sign of the way laws are changing to meet the challenge of new crimes. They were charged with exceeding authorized access to computer systems, computer fraud, and wire fraud. Behind those offenses was the theft of shares worth nearly $8 million.

Osowski and Tang accessed the system used by Cisco to manage stock options and found the control numbers used to track authorized stock-option dispersals. They were then able to create forged forms, which appeared to show they should be issued shares. They set up personal accounts at Merrill Lynch and faxed the forms to the company that was responsible for issuing the shares.

Three times they had shares moved to their personal accounts at Merrill Lynch. In the end, these added up to $7,868,637. When the government seized stock still in the accounts, it raised just over $5 million. An automobile and jewelry were also seized. In addition to 34 months each in prison, the two men agreed to pay restitution.

In 2002, a Computer Security Institute/FBI survey found financial losses from unauthorized insider access ranging from $1,000 to $5 million. The average loss was $275,000. To counter this, there is a move away from reusable passwords, which in practice, are seldom changed. Instead, single-use passwords are combined with cards that identify the user.

Rebecca Herold, a consultant with Nitigy, says: "It's good to see a trend in a decrease of reusable passwords." She admits that getting people to use one-time passwords is a challenge, but says that once they have experience, they "like (or at least accept) the way they work."

Cisco Systems in California is a leader in network systems and has developed a range of products to prevent unauthorized intrusions. Their Intrusion Detection System watches for changed patterns of behavior as well as using more conventional detection techniques.

The 1995 movie *Hackers*, staring Angelina Jolie (pictured), portrays the lives of young New York City hackers who become unwittingly involved in a high-stakes financial conspiracy with a large multinational corporation.

THE RISE OF EXTERNAL ATTACKS

Ms. Herold explains that there is a long way to go in improving security. Security people need to be in positions where they have real influence over policy. "I still remember being asked in 1995 why I wanted to be in a 'dead-end' job such as security. The person asking me this told me I could only be spending about four hours a day working on user IDs and access changes. They told me I should look into doing something with a more promising future, because they didn't think security would ever be a position that needed to be filled with the 'technical advances' being made. Okay, this person was an IT manager then, but is now a night-time manager at a convenience store," she says.

While survey results showed that external attacks were overtaking internal attacks, security experts warned about the dangers of complacency and the danger of relying on statistics. Writing in *Information Security Bulletin*, Dr. Eugene Schultz said: "Unfortunately, a lot of the confusion comes from the fact that some people keep quoting a 17-year-old FBI statistic that indicated that 80 percent of all attacks originated from the inside. At the time this statistic was first released, it was almost certainly valid—the computing world at that time consisted to a large degree of mainframes and stand-alone PCs… Today, we have a proliferation of network services (most notably the World Wide Web service) available to the entire Internet community—a truly target-rich environment for would-be attackers."

Dr. Schulz said that while the CSI/FBI survey showed outsider attacks outnumbering internal ones, he believed external attacks were being vastly underestimated. "I'd like to add that any statistics concerning security-related incidents and computer crime are suspect and should not be taken at face value. What is the main point here? Is it that we should ignore the insider threat in favor of the outsider threat? On the contrary. The insider threat remains the greatest single source of risk to organizations. But what I am saying is that it is important to avoid underestimating the external threat."

CYBER CRIME FACTS

- The most frequent and most costly security breaches are committed by authorized users.(Digital Research, Inc.)
- Authorized users, including employees, consultants, and business partners, commit 75% of all computer crime. (Digital Research, Inc.)

- Insider hacking represents 70% of all malicious attacks and causes $1 billion in damages each year to U.S. businesses. (*Business Week*)
- Thirty-six percent of users use their work computers to look for new jobs. (Vault.com 2000 Survey of Internet Use in the Workplace)
- Over 4.2 million Internet users visited eBay during one week, each visitor spending, on average, over 51 minutes at the site—all this while at work. (Weekly Internet Ratings for Nielsen/Netratings.com, January 12, 2001)
- 46.9% of workers spend at least 30 minutes during an average workday surfing non-work-related sites, with another 25% surfing up to 30 minutes. (Vault.com 2000 Survey of Internet Use in the Workplace)
- Seventy-nine percent of companies detected employee abuse of Internet access privileges. (Computer Security Institute, March 22, 2000)
- 54.2% of workers admit to being caught by their employer while surfing non-work-related sites. (Vault.com Internet Use Survey, Fall 2000)
- Forty-one percent of employers restrict or monitor their employees' Internet or e-mail use. (Vault.com Internet Use Survey, Fall 2000)

These nuggets were collected by Vericept Corporation, which specializes in systems that monitor and prevent network abuse. While staff use the Internet for non-work purposes, like shopping, employers are increasingly concerned about the effect on productivity, and this may be a firing offense, as may be the sending of inappropriate e-mails.

Business Under Attack

A new kind of robber needs a new kind of cop. Michael Morris is one of the new cops. Bored with his $96,000-a-year job with accountants Price Waterhouse (as it was then called), he packed it in and enrolled in the FBI Academy for a $2,000 monthly paycheck. When he got his man after a five-year investigation, he was hailed as the FBI's leading computer gumshoe. The robber in this high-tech cops-and-robbers story was Calvin Cantrell. A letter from him read aloud in a Dallas courtroom said, "My parents taught me good ethics, but I have departed from some of these, lost my way sometimes. I was 25 and living at home. No job, and no future.... All I ever really wanted was to work with computers." Cantrell did work with computers—those of some of the largest corporations in the world, but without authorization.

CALVIN CANTRELL AND THE PHONEMASTERS

Cantrell belonged to a gang the FBI called the Phonemasters. Their high-tech crimes began in a low-tech way with Dumpster diving. They collected old phone books and telephone system manuals that had been thrown away, and gained enough information to get into phone company systems. They were in the business of selling information. They broke into the networks of AT&T, British Telecom, Southwestern Bell, and Sprint. They got into the Nexis/Lexis databases and Dun and Bradstreet. They hacked into a cache of unpublished phone numbers at the White House and conspired to break into the FBI's National Crime Information Center (NCIC).

The Phonemasters had a price list: personal credit reports, $75; state

Left: Shawn Fanning, founder of Napster, the once-dominant Internet music-swapping service, which found itself under attack from the big music corporations. They saw Napster as aiding pirating, otherwise called intellectual property theft.

Information is valuable. Businesses and government agencies protect it, but criminals are increasingly turning to the Internet as a way into the vast databases of information that can be sold. Other criminals and unscrupulous corporations may be among the customers.

motor vehicle records, $25; FBI Crime Information Center records, $100. For $500, they would provide the address and phone number of any "celebrity or important person." The customers were private investigators, so-called information brokers, and, through middlemen, the Sicilian Mafia. Information was sold to someone in Canada, who transferred it to someone else in the United States, who sent it to another middleman in Switzerland, who then sold it to the Mafia.

Michael Morris first heard about the Phonemasters from a Dallas private investigator. He listened to the price list and persuaded the investigator to meet Cantrell while wired for sound. After listening to the tapes, the FBI put in a device that recorded the numbers dialed on Cantrell's line. It showed calls to many phone company numbers and two to unlisted numbers at the White House. However, the existing legal powers in 1994 were not enough to investigate this case.

Morris realized that he needed new powers to crack the case, and he was determined to get them. While tapping telephone lines for voice was allowed (with many restrictions), intercepting the impulses generated by computer modems was not. He wrote to the FBI's headquarters in Washington, D.C. and to the federal district court in Dallas. "It was," says Morris, "one of the hardest techniques to get approved, partly because it is so intrusive. The public citizen in me appreciates that. It took a lot of educating federal attorneys."

DEVELOPING NEW DETECTION EQUIPMENT

That was the legal issue. The other issue was getting equipment that would do the job. Morris worked with technicians at the FBI Quantico

Michael Morris took a big pay cut to enrol here at the FBI Academy to learn how to be an agent. He turned out to be no ordinary agent, but the man who has been called the FBI's leading computer gumshoe. His five-year investigation is a classic of cyber crime detection.

engineering lab to specify the equipment to convert the modem tones back into digital signals—technically, a difficult task.

While he waited for the equipment, another Phonemasters scam was uncovered. They created fake telephone numbers that forwarded calls to phone-sex lines in Germany. How the Phonemasters got people to call the numbers was never discovered, but Cantrell got a payment of $2,200 from Germany for generating the traffic. The Phonemasters also diverted some FBI field office lines to premium-rate numbers in Germany, Moldavia, and Hong Kong. That prank resulted in the FBI being billed $200,000 for illegal phone calls.

When Morris' $70,000 "magic box" arrived, it was installed in a leaky, unheated warehouse. This site was chosen because it was between Cantrell's home and the nearest telephone exchange. The 10 agents taking turns monitoring the data kept a tarp handy to protect the equipment when it rained. With enough data collected and analyzed, Cantrell and another man, Cory Lindsay, were convicted in 1999. Cantrell was jailed for two years, while Lindsay was sentenced to 41 months. Other members of the gang are still at large. Their activities are said to have added up to $1.85 million in business losses.

The significance of the Phonemasters case is that it introduced the concept of **wire-tapping** for data rather than voice. However, this is much more of a fishing expedition than with a voice intercept, where it is possible to quickly reject and destroy material that is not relevant to an inquiry. Furthermore, technological change often makes intercepts more difficult. Increasingly, even home computers use digital rather than analog modem signals and **encryption**.

RUSSIAN COMPUTER CRIMINALS

However, all the information in the world is no help if the cop cannot get the cuffs on the robber. This was the problem for Special Agents Marty Prewett and Michael Schuler. They knew the names of their men and they

Chelyabinsk in the foothills of the Ural Mountains remains an impoverished city in post-Communist Russia, a seemingly unlikely place to find hackers. But from here emerged two of the most significant cyber criminals to fall into the hands of the FBI.

THE FBI INVESTIGATES

- One espionage case generated enough data to fill the Library of Congress twice over.
- The increased use of encryption for faxes and cell phones, as well as computer communications, has placed a "tremendous burden" on the FBI's electronic surveillance technologies.
- Every increase in the size of computer hard drives increases the work of computer forensic investigators. Even if the disk is not full, every part of it has to be examined.
- In 2001, the FBI's Computer Analysis Response Team was expected to carry out 6,000 forensic examinations.
- Investigation of an extortion case required millions of Web sites to be sifted.

knew where they lived—in Chelyabinsk in the eastern foothills of Russia's Ural Mountains. Since the fall of Communism, organized crime has flourished in the former Soviet states, and well-educated, computer-literate men with poor prospects of reasonably paid jobs have turned to computer crime. Much of the intrusion into sensitive private and government databases around the world is traced to Russia.

Prewett and Schuler were investigating Russian computer intrusions directed at Internet Service Providers, e-commerce sites, and online banks in the United States. The hackers used their unauthorized access to the victims' computers to steal credit card information and other personal financial information. They often tried to **extort** money from the victims with threats to expose the sensitive data to the public or damage the victims' computers. Stolen credit card numbers were used to generate cash to pay for computer parts purchased from vendors in the United States.

Since the agents could not go to Russia and arrest them, they decided they would have to tempt them to the United States. Accordingly, they created a start-up computer security company named "Invita" in Seattle, Washington. Posing as Invita personnel, the FBI men contacted Vasiliy Gorshkov and another man, Alexey Ivanov, by e-mail and telephone. The Russians agreed to prove their skills by trying to hack into a computer system. They broke into the network without realizing that the FBI had provided it. Having demonstrated their hacking skills, Gorshkov and Ivanov agreed to visit Seattle to talk business.

THE CRIMINALS TAKE THE BAIT

Unsuspecting, the two arrived in Seattle for their meeting with Invita executives. It seemed to them to be going well—until they were arrested. Gorshkov and Ivanov were charged in the Western District of Washington with conspiracy and 19 additional crimes involving Speakeasy, Nara Bank, Central National Bank, Waco, and PayPal, the Internet payment site. A few days after the two men were arrested, the FBI obtained access via the Internet to two of the men's computers in Russia.

Data copied from the Russian computers provided the investigators with a wealth of evidence of the men's computer hacking and fraud. They had large databases of credit card information that was stolen from Internet Service Providers, like Lightrealm of Kirkland, Washington. Details of more than 56,000 credit cards were found on the two Russian computers. Stolen bank account numbers and other personal financial information regarding customers of online banking at Nara Bank and Central National Bank, Waco, were also found.

The conspirators had gained unauthorized control over numerous computers—including computers of a school district in St. Clair County, Michigan—and then used those compromised computers to commit a massive fraud involving PayPal and the online auction company eBay.

Gorshkov's programs created associated accounts at PayPal with random identities and stolen credit cards. Additional computer programs allowed the conspirators to control and manipulate eBay auctions. They acted as both seller and winning bidder in the same auction and then effectively paid themselves using the stolen credit cards.

THE PAIRGAIN HOAX

By comparison, the idea behind the PairGain hoax was simplicity itself. People logging on to financial bulletin boards hosted by Yahoo! and others got a tip that a Californian telecom equipment company was to be taken over. The Israeli buyer was to pay $1.35 billion. There was a link to an apparent news item at Bloomberg, the financial information service. PairGain stock rose by 31% on the NASDAQ Exchange. However, it was a hoax. Thousands of victims who bought shares as a result of the false tip lost large sums when the price collapsed. The perpetrator of the hoax had covered his tracks well, but not well enough to prevent investigators from tracing him through a web of e-mail addresses. The fake Bloomberg page was on a free site that looked like the real thing, and links took visitors to the real Bloomberg site. The person who had set up the fake site registered with a first name of "headlines" and a second name of "99." He also gave a Hotmail e-mail address.

Eventually, analysis of IP addresses—the numbers by which computers are identified—led to Gary Hoke, a PairGain employee in Raleigh, North Carolina. However, he had subsequently gotten "cold feet" and had never actually profited from his scheme.

INTERNET AUCTION FRAUD

Internet auctions have become among the most frequent scenes of cyber crimes. They range from major frauds, like selling fake pictures and upping the price by putting in "shill bids"—false offers made by an associate to push the price up. In one case, a fake painting was sold for $135,000, but most auction frauds are smaller.

For example, the Internet is a great way for a man to buy his daughter's birthday present if he lives a long way from the major stores. Reaching an auction site, he finds a Beanie Baby. It looks cute—just the right gift. It does not take long to confirm the purchase and put a money order in the mail. The Beanie Baby never arrives, but the money order is cashed.

That is the profile of a typical Internet fraud. Seven out of 10 victims are

At the height of the dot-com boom, prices of high-tech companies soared on the Nasdaq Exchange. An elaborate Internet scam sent the price of one company's stock up by 31%, but the hoaxer lost his nerve and did not take a profit.

men and three-quarters of them are between the ages of 20 and 50. Someone living in Alaska is three times more likely to be the victim than someone living in Maryland. The Internet Fraud Complaint Center that compiled these figures found that more than half of all complaints were about auctions and of those, 27% were about the nondelivery of Beanie Babies. Much Internet fraud is old tricks pulled in new ways. Mail-order scams have moved into cyberspace, and thieves have found a new way of disposing of what they have stolen.

Two Michigan men were charged, according to Associated Press (AP), with committing old-fashioned shoplifting with a high-tech twist—**fencing** thousands of dollars in stolen goods through the Internet auction site eBay. Police said the pair shoplifted $40,000 worth of goods from discount stores in

Dennis Moran, a 19-year-old hacker who used the handle "Coolio" in chat rooms, was once thought to be responsible for a series of Denial of Service attacks but eventually pleaded to three misdemeanors. He was sentenced to one year's incarceration and ordered to pay $15,000.

ONLINE AUCTION FRAUD

- Two-thirds of all reported Internet fraud concerns auctions.
- Complaints against individuals, as opposed to businesses, account for 84% of all complaints.
- Over 1.3 million transactions a day take place on Internet auction sites. Less than 1% of these transactions result in fraud.
- Of all reported Internet auction fraud, 34% of the victims do not know the gender of the person they are complaining about.
- Most items involved in Internet auction fraud fall into six major categories. Although Beanie Babies are the biggest by number, they are the smallest by value. The other five categories are video consoles/games/tapes, laptop computers, cameras/camcorders, desktop computers, and jewelry.
- Money orders or personal checks are the method of payment for 80% of the victims that reported Internet auction fraud.
- A typical fraudulent seller gives an e-mail address for contact, but if a physical address is given, it will probably be a P.O. Box address in the U.S. The e-mail address is likely to be at AOL, Yahoo!, or Hotmail.

Source: Internet Fraud Complaint Center

Michigan, Ohio, and Indiana, and then sold about half of it on eBay to buyers around the world.

A detective explained their technique: the two men would first buy something like a wheelbarrow that came in a large box. They would then empty the box, return to the store, and fill it with high price items, like digital cameras and radios. They would then pay for the "wheelbarrow" again and walk out of the shop with their loot. They then offered the stolen property on the Internet auction site.

"DON'T STEAL MUSIC"

Just when you think you have heard about every possible computer crime, someone invents a new gizmo and someone else applies it to crime. One young man walked into a store, Dallas Comp USA, listening to music on an iPod. He walked up to an Apple Mac and used a FireWire to plug the iPod into the computer, then copied $500 worth of Microsoft software. With the speed of the iPod, the 200 MB of software was transferred in less than a minute.

The iPod is designed for listening to music, but with 5 GB of storage, it can hold any computer file. A sticker on new iPods warns, "Don't steal music."

THE THIEVING GOES ON

The theft of private business information was highlighted in the 2002 CSI/FBI computer security survey. "Do you find the report of a $50-million loss due to the theft of proprietary information (the largest reported in the survey) implausible?" the report asks. "If you do, you simply don't read the business section of your newspaper closely enough. In July 2001, AP reported that Avant, a software company, was ordered to pay $182 million in restitution for stealing source code from Cadence, a competing firm, to settle one of Silicon Valley's longest running trade-secret theft cases."

In another case, two Chinese scientists and an American were arrested for stealing source code from a leading American company for a Beijing telecom company.

As with traditional crime, most of it is small-scale. It requires no more than average computer literacy. A problem for police is that even the Michigan men, who would once have sold the stolen goods in a local bar, were able to sell the merchandise around the world. That makes gathering evidence and recovering property more difficult.

Pirating of software, music, films, and books and the stealing of trade secrets is called intellectual property rights theft. As long ago as 1997, the American Society of Industrial Security put losses at $2 billion a month. Since then, faster connections have made it easier to download large music files and even films from the mushrooming number of sites. After Napster settled in the courts, the flow of pirated music has slowed only a little. The owners of intellectual property say it is their income and jobs that are threatened. Opponents point out that they do not see the global entertainment and media groups suffering.

In cyberspace, where everything is digital information, intellectual property is set to become a hot debate. It is predicted to become an even hotter issue than it was at the height of the Napster case.

Mike Winkler (left), of Compaq, shows off the iPaq personal audio player at its launch. While MP3 players like this are completely legal, music companies are worried that they facilitate the pirating of music. Others see them as simply a convenient way to listen to favorite groups.

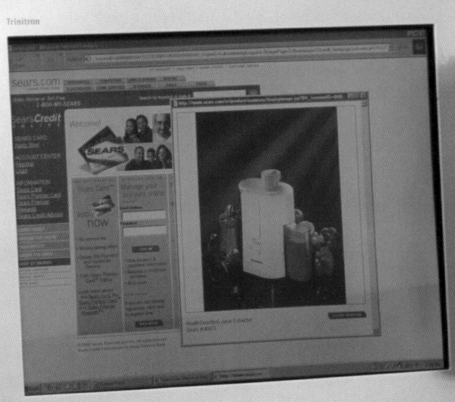

Virus Attack

There is one cyber crime every computer user has suffered from—a virus attack. These have the means of insidiously finding their way into our computers, beating down our "immune systems," and doing their damage, just like the common cold virus. The difference is that computer viruses are manmade with the intention of causing damage. When Robert Morris unleashed his worm in 1988, it brought half the Internet to a standstill. There were no defenses. The world was not expecting it, and there was no antivirus software to act as the immune system.

THE MORRIS WORM

Few people noticed the worm. The Internet was then restricted largely to universities and the defense and intelligence communities. Robert Morris, then aged 24, was a graduate student at Cornell. He released the Morris Worm accidentally, but said he had been influenced by John Brunner's book *Shockwave Rider.* This is about a gearhead warrior tring to overthrow a network-dependent government by attacking its information arteries.

Morris' first encounter with anything that could be called a computer was when his father brought home one of the Enigma code machines used by the Germans in World War II to encrypt messages before they were sent by radio. The British obtained a machine and analyzed how it worked, which helped them to decode these messages. Morris' father was chief scientist at the National Computer Security Center, part of the National Security Agency (NSA). Like most virus writers, Morris was well educated. The motivation of virus writers has puzzled researchers, who conclude

Left: Every computer user is likely to suffer a virus attack at some time. At the least, these are annoying, but some cause real damage, destroying valuable files and software. Sensible computer users use antivirus software and remain aware of potential weaknesses in their systems.

A German Enigma encoding machine, like the one Morris' father brought home from work and showed his son. A captured machine helped the British to decode secret German messages and their success probably shortened World War II.

DENIAL OF SERVICE ATTACKS

As people have become more "streetwise" about avoiding viruses and protection software has become more common, another form of attack has become more prevalent. Distributed denial of service attacks crash Web servers or, at best, slow traffic to a crawl. A DDOS attack floods the server with an overwhelming number of requests that need a response. DDOS attacks are more recent than hacking or virus writing and were first investigated in 1999. Many major e-businesses, including Yahoo!, have been attacked, as have government sites. The source and motivation of DDOS attacks remains unclear, as it is difficult to find out who is behind them. In many cases, the attackers use fake IP addresses, which hide the real source of the attack.

simply, "Most will grow out of it." Morris was brought before a court in one of the first major trials under the Computer Fraud and Abuse Act of 1986 and sentenced to three years probation and 400 hours of community service. He was also fined $10,000. The word "hacker" came into common use.

A series of viruses have followed, some minor irritants and some causing serious damage to computer systems. The impact of viruses has grown along with the Internet itself. In 1999, when the Melissa virus was released into the "wild," there were 100 million Internet users in the United States. By the end of 2003, that figure is expected to reach 177 million and more than 500 million worldwide. That means more people can reach more people by e-mail and, thus, the viruses will spread faster.

THE MELISSA VIRUS

Just six days after the Melissa virus was released on March 26, 1999, causing an estimated $80 million worth of damage, 31-year-old David L.

Richard Smith retired from the software company he helped to create and devoted himself to his hobby—Internet security. He has found bugs in e-mail software and Web browsers, and he fingered David L. Smith (no relation), the author of the Melissa virus.

Smith was arrested in New Jersey. A serious view was taken of the attack, signaled by the people who lined up to comment. Attorney General Janet Reno said, "In light of society's increasing dependence on computers, the [Justice] Department will vigorously investigate and prosecute computer crimes that threaten our computer infrastructure."

U.S. Attorney Robert J. Cleary said, "The Melissa virus demonstrated the danger that business, government, and personal computer users everywhere face in our technological society. Far from being a mere nuisance, Melissa infected computers and disabled computer networks throughout North America. There is a segment in society that views the unleashing of computer viruses as a challenge, a game. Far from it, it is a serious crime."

And New Jersey State Attorney General John Farmer, Jr. said, "Computer criminals may think that they operate in a new frontier without boundaries, where they won't be caught. Obviously, that's not true. We've

The Chernobyl virus struck hard at City Hall, Fulton, New York. Here, Scott Palocy, administrative aide to the mayor, is working on one of the virus-hit machines. Normally, repairs after a virus do not involve dismantling a computer.

VIRUSES AND HOW TO DEAL WITH THEM

A virus is a program that is loaded onto your computer without your knowledge and which runs against your wishes. Viruses can replicate themselves. Even a simple virus is dangerous because it can stop the system by using all available space.

A macro virus is carried normally by Microsoft Word files. The effects can be avoided by disabling macros when downloading files from the Internet. Antivirus software scans incoming files. However, regular updating is necessary to avoid newly developed viruses.

To avoid virus infection, never open e-mail attachments from anyone you do not know. Beware particularly of extensions like .exe. Think twice before opening an attachment on any forwarded e-mail. Always scan floppy disks that have been in any other computer, including those from your best friend.

VIRUS TIMELINE

1949: Theory of self-replicating programs developed.

1981: First "wild" viruses released; they spread on Apple II computers via pirated games.

1983: Formal definition of a computer virus—a program that can affect other programs by modifying them in such a way as to include a copy of itself.

1986: Two programmers release a virus that infects floppy disks and gives them the volume label "© Brain."

1987: The common virus Jerusalem is unleashed; activated every Friday the 13th, it affects both .exe and .com files and deletes any programs run that day.

1988: Morris Worm is introduced.

1990: Symantec launches Norton AntiVirus, one of the first widely available commercial defenses.

1991: The first polymorphic virus in the wild; polymorphic viruses change their appearance with each new infection.

1992: There are 1,330 known viruses in existence; first media hype predicts Michelangelo virus will crash five million computers; fewer than 10,000 go down.

1993: The first hoax virus warns that opening e-mail will erase the entire hard disk; regular hoaxes ever since.

1999: Melissa virus is introduced, the fastest-spreading to date.

2000: The "Love Bug" virus is introduced; Stages, the first virus with a false .txt extension, is introduced, making it easier to lure recipients into opening it.

2001: Kournikova virus succeeds by offering pictures of the tennis star (pictured).

Source: infoplease.com

Onel de Guzman (left), the suspected author of the "I love you" virus, never admitted more than that he might have accidentally released it. The Philippines government dropped all charges against him, but it is unlikely he would have been convicted under the law as it then stood.

responded by breaking down traditional borders among federal, state, county, and local law enforcement. In this case, it helped us to make an arrest in less than a week."

The Melissa virus appeared on thousands of e-mail systems disguised as an important message from a colleague or friend. The virus was designed to send an infected e-mail to the first 50 e-mail addresses on the users' mailing lists. It therefore proliferated rapidly. Disrupting computer networks by overloading e-mail servers, it resulted in the shutdown of networks and costly repairs.

David Smith used a stolen America Online (AOL) account and his own account with a local Internet Service Provider to post an infected document on an "alt.sex" Internet newsgroup. The posting contained a message enticing readers to download and open the document in the hope of finding passwords to adult-content Web sites. Opening and downloading the message caused the Melissa virus to infect the victims' computers.

Part of the success of the Melissa virus had to do with the message in the e-mail: "Here is that document you asked for...don't show anyone else;-)."

THE "LOVE BUG" VIRUS

Two years later, the same technique was used again with the enticing message, "I love you." The so-called "love bug" virus was traced to a 27-year-old man in the Philippines. It had spread around the world in days. The message was irresistible to millions, including people at the Pentagon, the CIA headquarters, and the Houses of Parliament in London, England.

Sarah Gordon, a researcher at IBM's Thomas J. Watson Research Center, says most virus writers are intelligent, have good relationships with their parents and other young people, and generally are normal in tests for ethical development. Among the justifications she has found are:

"If my code was used to damage someone's computer, that is the responsibility of the person who's (sic) immature behavior has resulted in damage. Open your mind, and expand your horizons...it's a huge world out there, if you can just get over your fears." And "...this is nauseating...you feel you have the right to censor and condemn the creativity of young, brilliant minds. You fear what you don't understand…."

She says that most young virus writers grow out of it, but she has also identified an older and more technically competent group. She calls them "new-age virus writers" who operate openly and consider virus writing to be

Virus fighting is a 24-hour job. Here at Network Associates in Slough, England, the team worked to find a cure for the "love bug." Many computers are programed to check for antivirus software updates to counteract new viruses every day.

a form of research or self-expression. She doubts if tough legal penalties will work: "Those that continue writing and making viruses available to the general public will be seen as 'irresponsible' at best, and criminal at worst. That said, it is interesting to note that while some have argued for stronger legal action, research into adolescent at-risk behavior finds that youths are not significantly motivated by fear of legal reprisal or involvement with the criminal justice system. They are more likely to be influenced by peers, family, and significant others whom they like and respect. Fear of the law does not appear to be a major de-motivator for many virus writers, and it appears that for now, the community continues to play itself out over and over again. Until we begin to tackle the root causes of virus-writer motivation, this will continue to be the case; a multidisciplinary approach is required to solve a multifaceted problem. Anything less is oversimplification."

THE TRUTH ABOUT VIRUSES

Just how much damage a virus causes is a matter of dispute. According to the organization Computer Economics, the cost of malicious-code attacks in 2001 was $13.2 billion. This was down from $17.1 billion in 2000, the year of the Love Bug. Others say these figures are garbage. They claim that the figures are impossible to estimate and that there are a lot of vested interests in the computer security and antivirus business who want to talk up the threat to boost their own business.

In researching this book, I have found a mass of figures produced by experts in their fields, which appear to have been randomly generated. The one figure I could not find was the value of the worldwide computer security business.

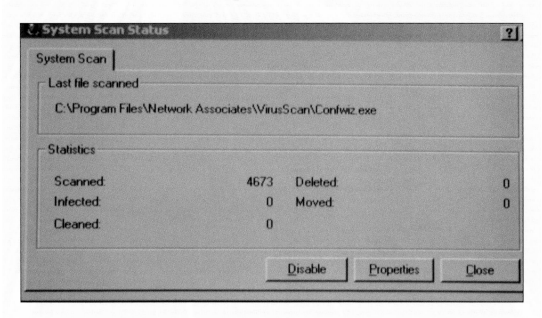

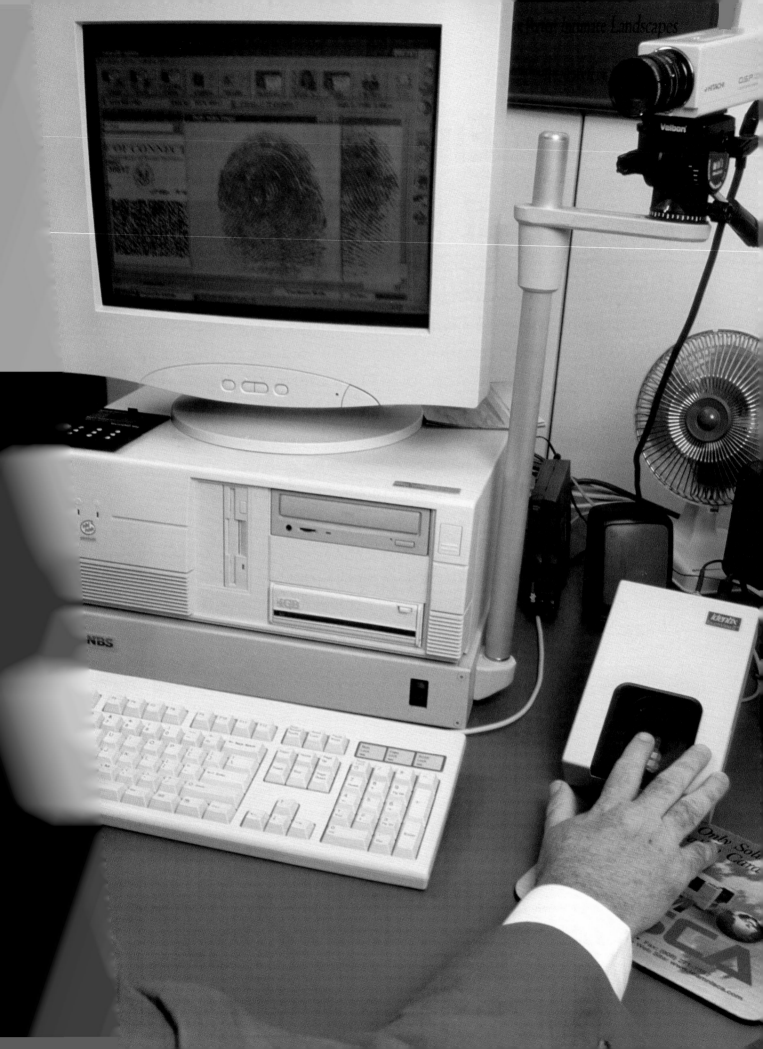

Law Enforcement and Security

Cyber crime is like an iceberg. Most of it is hidden because businesses and organizations are reluctant to admit they have been hit. Asked why they had not called the law enforcement agencies, 9 out of 10 said they were worried about bad publicity. Three-quarters thought competitors would use the information to their advantage. Two out of three said civil rather than criminal law seemed to offer the best remedy. And half said they were unaware that they could report the attack as a crime. These figures come from the CSI/FBI 2002 survey, which shows that, although most cases are not reported, the proportion in which police are asked to investigate is rising. At the same time, there is a perception that the attack is increasingly likely to come from the outside.

WHO ARE THE CYBER CRIMINALS?

There is nothing new about businesses hiding crime. No one wants to tell their customers or shareholders that they have failed to stop an accountant from transferring money into a private account. Shop owners are happy to take a shoplifter to court, but are much more reluctant to deal with employees who steal. These people are often fired, while the managers talk about "shrinkage," a **euphemism** that means loss of stock because of inside and outside theft.

An online trader, who depends on customers having the confidence to

Left: When security really matters, passwords are not enough. Too many people use something obvious, stick the password under a keyboard, or simply give it to a colleague. Here, fingerprint recognition is used to verify the user's identity.

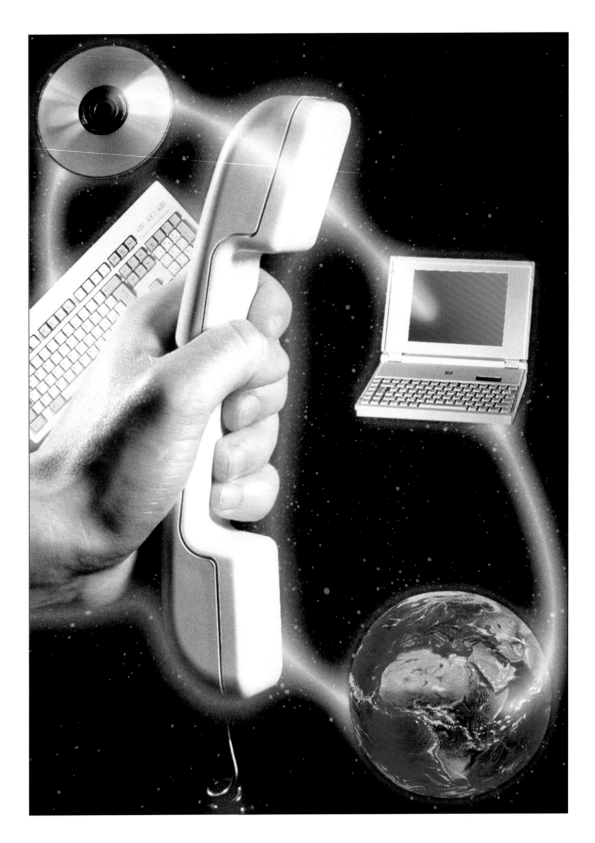

Internet technology and the World Wide Web mean that determined hackers and cyber criminals from anywhere in the world can access highly sensitive information and use it to their advantage.

SYSTEM ATTACK

Organizations and companies were asked what were likely sources of attacks on their systems. Most thought they might be hit in several ways.

LIKELY SOURCES OF ATTACK

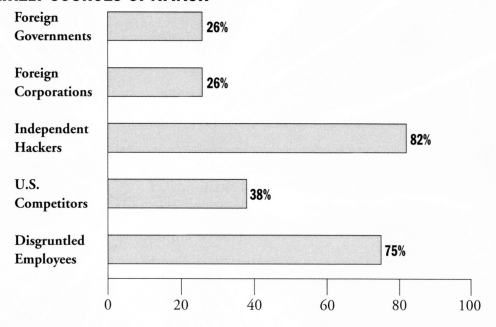

Source: Computer Security Institute 2002

provide credit card details, feels vulnerable to any admission that its computer security is less than 100 percent effective.

NEW WAYS TO MAKE SYSTEMS SECURE

Amid all these suspect statistics, where do the companies think the threat is coming from? The CSI/FBI survey asked about likely sources of attack—independent hackers, disgruntled employees, U.S. competitors, foreign corporations, or foreign governments. The most surprising thing is that when the three industrial espionage categories are added together, espionage comes out top (see chart).

In light of the often-vague threats to businesses and other organizations, computer security has itself become big business. Computer security businesses are growing rapidly, and the consultant arms of the huge international accountancy firms are among the biggest players. Preventing intrusions in the first place is better than the incomplete cure offered by a later police investigation. Just as we protect our homes with locks, burglar alarms, and fire alarms, companies are spending more on securing their computer systems. As with street crime and burglary, there is the fear-of-crime factor. Is the threat overestimated?

Computers are vulnerable because people use them. Passwords are often not secure because they get written down, often on a note stuck inside a desk. Or the password is something simple and easy for another person to guess, like a birthday or the name of a pet. The theory is that passwords should be changed at least every 30 days. However, this can cause irritation and anger, which is often vented on the computer staff by people who find they have been barred from the system. Simply, people have too many PIN numbers and passwords to remember these days and find that they have to write at least some of them down.

The trend now is to augment the password (something you know) with something you have, such as an authorization card. Even if someone gets hold of the password, it is useless without the card. Until card readers are built into home computers, however, this will not work for organizations like Internet banks, which require high security. They take the "something you know" idea further by asking personal questions that someone who has stolen a diary with the password written in it will not be able to answer. You might, for example, be asked for a memorable date or your favorite book.

Card access, like passwords, is far from foolproof. Cards may be lost or stolen. And most people are reluctant to let a security door slam in the face of someone who is following clutching an armful of files.

In Germany, Kim Schmitz was convicted of hacking into corporate computer systems and stealing telephone calling-card numbers. Afterwards, he lived a flamboyant lifestyle and claimed to have made millions of dollars from computer security and Internet businesses. In 2002, aged 28, he was again arrested, for insider dealing and fraud.

BIOMETRICS

To avoid the security problems of human shortcomings, organizations that need to be really secure are moving to biometrics. This means identifying some personal characteristic of an individual—fingerprint, voice, keystroke pattern, or the pattern of the retina of the eye. One in 20 of the respondents to the CSI survey uses biometrics. Voice recognition is built into the operating system of Apple Mac computers. The picture shows hand readers, which recognize the characteristics of an individual's hand. They are used to ensure that only authorized people can enter a secure area.

COMPUTER FORENSICS

Like banks and other traditional businesses, computer-based ventures spend billions on keeping intruders out and trying to stop disgruntled employees from putting their fingers in the till or taking revenge over a perceived injustice.

Police around the world are finding that countering computer crime needs news skills, new laws, and new techniques. Computer forensics—examining computers for traces of how they have been used—is one of the fastest-growing areas of criminal investigation. It has had to spread resources thinly because calls for computer investigations have become routine. In a recent case of a schoolgirl who went missing on her way home

Credit cards should be used with care on the Internet, as they should be anywhere else. The advice is to look for the locked padlock symbol in the browser window that indicates a secure site and to deal only with well-known and reputable companies.

Germany's national police squad, the BKA, uncovered an international pedophile ring. Operation ARTUS, coordinated by Interpol, involved police in Canada, Finland, France, Germany, Japan, the Netherlands, Spain, Sweden, Switzerland, the United Kingdom, and the United States.

from school in England, her computer was examined to see if she had made any contacts over the Internet.

Hamid Ghodse, president of the International Narcotics Control Board, warned in his 2001 annual report that, "Cyber crime is easy to commit. It requires few resources and can be committed in one country by a person sitting safely in another. It is difficult to fight both the criminals and their crimes in this 'virtual' environment, where national boundaries are irrelevant and personal risk to the criminals and the likelihood of detection are greatly reduced."

Organized crime has adapted to minimize risk. The traditional crime family with a Mafia-style "capo" at its head and a rigid hierarchy is giving

INTERPOL ADVICE

Interpol has responded to questions it is frequently asked about computer information security by making a number of recommendations. First of all, employers are advised that staff should be aware of (and also accept) the difference between "nice to know" and "need to know" information, meaning that employees should have access only to the information they need to do their jobs effectively.

To secure an Internet connection against hacking, data spying, and data altering, Interpol recommends using a firewall. In addition, an Intrusion Detection System (IDS) should be installed to protect against internal attacks.

An Incident Handling System (IHS) should be prepared to minimize damage and losses after an incident. If a company with an IDS realizes a hacker is attacking the system, it is prepared to handle the incident. This will involve disconnecting the system from the Internet and making a full backup so that evidence (for example, IP addresses and log-in times) can be collected. Interpol also recommends notifying the police if there is a serious threat or damage.

Stand-alone computers can be protected through the use of system and screensaver passwords. No one should write passwords under their keyboards, and passwords should be changed frequently. As well as using encryption to protect important and confidential information, Interpol recommends the use of alarm systems and floppy-drive locks.

Viruses should be protected against by using antivirus software. Beware of downloading information that comes from unknown sources and e-mails sent by unknown persons.

way to new structures that are much more difficult to penetrate. These groupings have a fluid network of cells in which national identity is less important than the cell's function and skills. They do not respect national borders, but minimize risks and maximize profits by working across several countries. Investigators can no longer presume that a particular criminal activity falls entirely under their jurisdiction. Like legitimate business, organized crime is going global.

COORDINATING THE FIGHT AGAINST CYBER CRIME

Police and security agencies, unlike the criminals, are edging slowly toward a more global approach. The biggest step has been the Council of Europe's Convention on Cybercrime (see Chapter One).

The difficulties of coordinating the fight against cyber crime on both sides of the Atlantic are small compared with those in other parts of the world. One survey found that two out of three countries had not updated their laws to deal with cyber crime. Even where they had, the laws were limited in their effect.

If the laws were harmonized, however, the problems would not end there. Colombian and U.S. agents who arrested 30 suspected drug traffickers found the gang had sophisticated computer communications. Messages were fed through a computer on a ship off the Mexican coast. A raid on the ship would have caused huge problems of jurisdiction for investigators.

National coordination of the various law enforcement and intelligence agencies involved in the fight against cyber crime is hard enough. In the U.S., the National Infrastructure Protection Center (NIPC) has been set up. While located at the FBI, it brings together representatives of the intelligence community and other federal agencies. Canada, the United Kingdom, and Australia also have representatives at the NIPC.

Ron Dick, the NIPC director, explains that it "functions in a task-force-like way, coordinating investigations in a multitude of jurisdictions, both domestically and internationally. This is essential due to the trans-

One approach to improving the security of credit card payments over the Internet is to have card readers attached to computers. This overcomes the problem of the theft of card numbers that can be used without the card being physically present.

Robert S. Mueller became FBI Director in 2001. He was previously U.S. Attorney for the Northern District of California, although he had simultaneously been Acting Deputy Attorney General of the U.S. Department of Justice before taking up his new post.

national nature of cyberintrusions. As NIPC coordinates a myriad of investigative efforts within the FBI, it is not unlike the way the air traffic control system manages the stream of aircraft traffic across the United States and around the world."

While NIPC is primarily concerned with computer intrusion, the U.S. Secret Service, founded in 1865 to combat currency counterfeiting, has found a new role in fighting cyber crime. Today, the threat to financial order comes less from illicit printing presses than from criminals with computers who can move money around the world with a few keystrokes.

THE CYBER CRIME DIVISION

Robert S. Mueller, who became the FBI Director in 2001 under the Bush administration, admitted that there had been flaws in the coordination of the fight against cyber crime when he presented his 2003 budget to Congress. He announced the formation of a new Cyber Crime Division dedicated to preventing and responding to high-tech and computer crimes, which, he said, "terrorists around the world are increasingly exploiting to attack America and its allies. Our old structure was fractured and not well coordinated. This change will bring together various cyberinitiatives and programs under one umbrella, so we are better focused, organized, and coordinated in working with our public- and private-sector partners to protect our nations."

Around the world, law enforcers are struggling to keep pace with the growth of the Internet and the increase in crime that comes with it. That said, the vast majority of Web users are never victims of cyber crime. Most have become aware of the dangers and take steps to protect themselves. They use antivirus software and are careful about opening e-mail attachments. Credit card details can just as easily be stolen in a restaurant (probably more easily), and most users now look for the locked padlock symbol in the browser that indicates personal information is being encrypted. We are becoming more streetwise on the information superhighway.

GLOSSARY

Biometrics: use of physical characteristics, such as fingerprints and voice, to identify users

Cyber crime: crime involving the use of networked computers

Disgruntled: discontented

Embezzle: to appropriate something fraudulently for one's own use

Encryption: conversion of data into a secure code

Euphemism: the substitution of an agreeable or inoffensive expression for one that may offend or suggest something unpleasant

Extort: to obtain something from a person by force, intimidation, or undue or illegal power

Fence (v.): to sell stolen property

Firewall: software that defends a system from unauthorized use or access

Hacker: someone who is a computer expert or someone who gains illegal access to computer systems

Internet Service Provider (ISP): business that provides customers with access to the Internet

Interpol: an association of national police forces that promotes cooperation and mutual assistance in apprehending international criminals and criminals who flee abroad to avoid justice

Intrusion detection system (IDS): software designed to detect misuse of a system

Jurisprudence: a system or body of law

Password: a data string used to verify the identity of a user

Phreaker: a person who hacks telephone systems

Restitution: a making good of or giving an equivalent for some injury

Wire-tapping: interception of communications

Xenophobic: having an unreasonable fear of what is foreign and especially of people of foreign origin

CHRONOLOGY

1970:   Arpanet, a military research network, is founded.

1971:   First e-mail program is used on Arpanet.

1972:   John Draper (Cap'n Crunch) finds that a toy whistle in a cereal box gives free access to telephone networks; "phreaking" becomes a craze.

1980:   Arpanet crashes because of the accidental distribution of a virus.

1983:   Internet is founded, with the Arpanet split into military and civilian sections.

1984:   The word "cyberspace" is coined by William Gibson in his novel *Neuromancer*.

1986:   "Cuckoo's Egg" Internet espionage case uncovered; Robert Morris' worm is unleashed in the "wild"; it causes a large part of the still-small Internet to crash.

1989:   Kevin Mitnick is convicted of stealing software and codes for long-distance phone lines; Tim Berners-Lee at the Cern high-energy physics lab in Geneva develops an early stage of what will become the World Wide Web; the first Computer Emergency Response Team (CERT) is formed because of concerns following the Morris worm.

1991:   Tim Berners-Lee publishes computer code for the World Wide Web; Kevin Poulsen, Ronald Austin, and Justin Paterson are charged with gaining control of a radio station's phone lines to win major prizes.

1994:   The Datastream Cowboy, Richard Price, described as the greatest threat to U.S. security, turns out to be a 16-year-old music student in London; hackers, directed from Russia, break into Citibank computers and transfer more than $10 million from accounts; all but $400,000 is recovered; Kevin Mitnick is arrested for a second time and charged with stealing credit card numbers; U.S. Defense Department computers are attacked 250,000 times.

1999: Melissa virus causes havoc worldwide; its writer, David L. Smith, is arrested in New Jersey within days; a fake Bloomberg news page is created as part of a scheme to boost the shares of a telecom equipment company, PairGain; Amazon and Yahoo! are almost overwhelmed by denial of service attacks; "Love Bug" becomes the most famous virus to date; French court rules that Yahoo! must block French users from accessing Nazi memorabilia on its auction site; Napster suspends its service because of litigation over intellectual property rights, and later comes back as a subscription service.

FURTHER INFORMATION

Useful Web Sites

In the world of the Internet, change is rapid. These links will help you get the latest cyber crime information. Although the sites listed are reliable, remember they primarily represent one viewpoint. For example, to get a balanced view of a government proposal on data tapping, you might also want to see what a civil liberties organization has to say.

Information from the Web needs to be carefully evaluated. Unlike a library, no selection has been made. In cyberspace, damaging gossip sits side-by-side with reliable facts and thoughtful analysis. Search engines (http//:www.google.com is currently the best) will find up-to-the minute information. When looking for people, put the names in quotation marks (for example, "Kevin Mitnick") to find the exact name.

Official and government Web sites
U.S. government's main information site, with details of law, policy, and cases: www.cybercrime.gov/

Internet Fraud Complaints Center: www1.ifccfbi.gov/index.asp

U.S. Department of Justice: www.usdoj.gov

The FBI: www.fbi.gov/

Interpol: www.interpol.int/

Council of Europe Cybercrime Convention: www.coe.int/portalT.asp

American Civil Liberties Union: www.aclu.org/

Civil liberties in Europe: www.statewatch.org/

Computer security Web sites
Computer security research center of the National Institute of Standards and Technology: vil.nai.com/VIL/default.asp

Computer Security Institute (produces the annual CSI/FBI computer security survey): www.gocsi.com/

The encyclopedia of computer security: www.itsecurity.com/

Other Web sites

For a different perspective, a Ukrainian site is devoted to cyber crime: www.crime-research.org/eng/

For cyber crime news on the Internet written by professional journalists, try: http://zdnet.com.com and http://www.infoworld.com/. Also try newspaper and broadcasting sites such as http://www.cnn.com and http://www.nytimes.com.

For Spanish language material: www.elpais.es; or, www.dailyearth.com

To find out what computer jargon means: whatis.techtarget.com/

To obtain virus information from one of the main suppliers of antivirus software, try Symantec, one of the leaders: securityresponse.symantec.com/

About the Author

Andrew Grant-Adamson is a journalist who became interested in computers when working as an industrial reporter and in 1976 taught himself to use a Commodore Pet, one of the first "personal" computers. He now lives in the English countryside and teaches new media journalism at City University, London.

INDEX

Page numbers in *italics* refer to illustrations and captions

antivirus software 65, 71, *74*, 85
Apple Computers 25, 29
Arpanet 23

Berners-Lee, Tim 13
Bevan, Matthew 33–4
Beyond Hope Convention *27*
"Billion-Dollar Bubble" 40–4
biometrics 82
businesses
    concealing crime 77
    external threat 47
    information theft from 51–63
    insider threat 37–49

Cantrell, Calvin 51–4
Chelyabinsk *55*, 56
Chernobyl virus *69*
Cisco Systems 44, *45*
Clarke, Richard *21*
Cleary, Robert J. 68
Cray, Seymour 23
credit cards 12, *19*, 26, 56, 57–8, *83*, *87*, 89
Cuckoo's Egg 18, 29–30
Cybercrime Convention 17, 20, 86

databases 51–63
Datastream Cowboy 30–3, *31*
DDOS (distributed denial of service) attacks 18, 67
death penalty 12–14
Department of Defense 21
Dick, Ron 86
Draper, John 25
drug trafficking 26
Dumpster diving 26, 51

eBay 57, 58
Ellis, Steven *15*
embezzlement 43
employees
    dismissed 37–40
    fraud by 40–4
Enigma machine 65, *66*
Equity Funding 40–4
extortion 56

Fanning, Shawn *50*
Farmer, John, Jr. 69
Federal Bureau of Investigation (FBI) 18, 25, 26, 34, 52–3, 56
fingerprint recognition *77*
firewall 85
forensics 40, *42*, 56, 83–6
fraud 40–4
    online auctions 58–61

Free Software Foundation 23
Freeh, Louis J. *16*, 17, 18

gambling *11*
Ghodse, Hamid 84
Gorshkov, Vasiliy 57
Gray, Raphael *19*
Guzman, Onel de *72*

hackers 12, 17, *19*, 23–35, *46*, 56, 67, *78*
Hackers 46
hacktivism 17–18, 35
Herold, Rebecca 44–7
Hoffman, William D. 40

identity theft 26
industrial espionage 80
information warfare 21
insider threat 17, 37–49
insurance fraud 40–4
intellectual property theft *51*, 63
Internet 11–12, 14–17, 26, 47
    auctions 57, 58–61
    traffic on 13
Interpol 85
Ivanov, Alexey 57

Jobs, Steve 25, 29, *29*
Johnston, Michael T. 26
juveniles 26–8, *28*

Kelly, Raymond 17
Kournikova virus 71
Kuji *31*, 33–4

law enforcement 77–89
Lindsay, Cory 54
Lloyd, Tim 40
loop-carrier systems 26–8
Love Bug 71, *72*, *73*, *74*, 75

Mafia 52
Massachusetts Institute of Technology 23
Melissa virus 18, 67–73
Michelangelo virus 71
Mitnick, Kevin 18, *32*, 34–5
modems 53
money laundering *11*
Moran, Dennis *60*
Morris, Michael 51, 52–4, *53*
Morris, Robert 65–7
Morris Worm 65–7, 70
Mueller, Robert S. *88*, 89
music, theft of *51*, 62, *63*

Napster *51*, 63
National Infrastructure Protection Center (NIPC) 86–9

Olsen, Glen 40
Operation Solar Sunrise 30
organized crime 26, 84–6
Osowski, Geoffrey 44

Packham, Bob 14
PairGain 58
passwords 30, 39, 44, *77*, 80, 85
PayPal 57
pedophiles 15–17, *84*
Penrose, Roy *14*
Phonemasters 18, 51–4
pirating *51*, 63, *63*
policing cyber space 12–17, 20
pornography 15
Prewett, Marty 54–8
Pryce, Richard 33–4

Reno, Janet 68
revenge attacks 37–40

sabotage 39–40
Schmitz, Kim *81*
Schuler, Michael 54–8
Schultz, Dr Eugene 47
security 25, 44–7, 77, 79–82, 85, 86
sensitive intrusions 21
shoplifting 60–1, 77
Smith, David L. 67–8, *68*
Smith, Richard *68*
Stallman, Richard 23
Steffen, Roswell 43
Stern, Donald K. 27, *28*
Stoll, Clifford 30

Tang, William 44
telephone systems 26–8
telephone tapping 53–4
telephones, free calls 25, 29
Tenebaum, Ehud 30
terrorists 18
theft
    information 51–63
    intellectual property *51*, 63
    music *51*, 62, *63*
Thompson, Ken 23

Unix 23

viruses 18, 65–75, 85
    dealing with 70–1
voice recognition 82

Walton, Greg 37–9
War Games 23–4, *24*
wire tapping 53–4
World Wide Web *9*, 13, 47, *78*
Wozniak, Steve 25, 29